The Bride Finder

8 GOALS FOR WINNING SOULS

ALLEN CHAPIN

NURTURE
PUBLISHERS

Nurture Publishers

ACKNOWLEDGMENTS

I would like to acknowledge the following people who have helped make this book possible:

- *Angela... for being my bride— truly exemplifying the Bride of Christ in a tangible way that I can see every day, and cheering me on to be and do all God has in store for me.*

- *Alex and Austin... for the incredible young men of God you are and the amazing examples you set. May you invite and lead many people to be a part of Christ's Bride throughout your life.*

- *Annese Chapin and Karen Chapin... for sharing your editing skills freely in order that many oth-*

ers may read without all the glaring distractions, and thereby be more easily inspired to lead many, many more to be a part of Christ's Bride.

• *All those who served as a part of my very first official launch team, too many to name... for helping get this book in the hands of more people so that we can reach more people to be the Bride of Christ.*

• *You, the reader... for investing your time— and maybe even your money— in this book, as well as sharing it with others. You have entrusted me with the gift of your time, and I am grateful for your confidence. May you find in these pages the initial reward of your investment: the inspiration and motivation you needed to move you forward.*

• *And most importantly, Lord Jesus... for inviting me to be a part of Your family, and then giving me the privilege of inviting others to be welcomed into the family. I am forever grateful!*

CONTENTS

INTRODUCTION

She walked into the lobby of the all-guys dorm on the campus of the university we attended during the first week we were there, and she *definitely* caught my attention. Long, beautiful, blonde curls and blue eyes like pools of water that you could just dive into. I can still remember to this day what she was wearing. I didn't know that day that she would one day say "yes" to my proposal and then become my bride for all these years. I just knew I wanted to meet her, and I wanted to get to know her.

Now to be clear, I didn't go to that Christian university seeking a wife. However, I did believe that it was possible the Lord would bring a young lady into my life while I was there who would want to spend the rest of her life serving Him alongside me. It was more than a matter of age and stage. It seemed like perhaps it might be part of His plan. He knew I would need someone in life who could help me and whom I could help.

Parents know that kind of stuff about their kids. I'm sure my parents knew it about me, though they were kind enough not to say to my face, "Dude, you really need to find a wife. It is NOT good for man to be alone."

So I'm not that surprised when I read in Genesis Chapter 24 that Abraham was aware of the fact that his son Isaac needed a wife. And like any good, loving, mostly well-meaning parent, Abraham wanted to help the process along. It was actually the way marriage relationships were established in that day and time. You didn't just turn 18, go to college, find yourself, find a spouse, and then hope to live out a fairy tale ending. Your parents determined you were ready and then found a wife who you would choose to love and with whom you would spend the rest of your life.

I know that sounds archaic and insensitive in our current westernized context, but I believe there is greater truth to be found in this story captured for us in Genesis that relates to those of us who call ourselves followers of Christ... perhaps even more than was noticed at first glance:

— In this story, we find the love of a father for his son. It's the love of a father who knows what his son most longs for and desires: a relationship that will last with someone he can love and who will love him in return.

— In this story, we also find a servant who loves his master so deeply that, at his master's request, he accepts the one assignment to find what the master's son desires.

Sound familiar? It should. Before Jesus returned to Heaven, He shared His Father's request with His servants: "Go into all the world and [find My Son a Bride.]"

You may have read it differently in various translations of Scripture, but that's the heart of it. You see, the Church at large is known as the Bride of Christ. In the analogy from Scripture, Christ is the Groom, and those of us who give our lives to Him become His Bride. In fact, the great celebration in Heaven when all believers arrive there together is even called the "marriage supper."

So, in essence, the Great Commission of Matthew 28:19-20, Mark 16:15-16, and Acts 1:8 is really a call for those of us who serve our Heavenly Master to become "Bride finders." The request of our Master— like Abraham to his servant— is simple: "Go find My Son a bride."

Now, that thought might scare you a little. You may think to yourself, "I'm no evangelist like Billy Graham, or Greg Laurie, or Kirk Cameron. I'm no preacher like those guys on TV who preach to thousands and people respond when they ask them to give their lives to Jesus. I'm just an average Jack or Jane. I'm a truck driver, or a housewife, or a student." Don't worry. That is precisely why I am writing this book.

To me, one of the most amazing points of the story found in Genesis 24 is that Abraham's servant wasn't really sure he could do what was being asked of him. He even asked Abraham, "But what if I can't...?" Maybe you've listened to your own fair share of sermons about witnessing— that is, sharing your faith with others—

and wondered to yourself, "You make it sound so easy, Preacher. But what if I can't?"

What if you *can*? What if someone gave you a pattern for how to help the people around you in life become the Bride of Christ? I believe that is exactly what God did for us when He inspired Genesis 24 to be written.

Oh, I believe it is an actual event that took place thousands of years ago. I believe Abraham, the servant, Isaac, and Rebekah are all real people, and that this is part of their true, historical account. But I also believe that woven throughout this factual, historical account are powerful, transformational truths we can apply to our lives these thousands of years later which will help us become *Bride Finders* in our own rights.

So do yourself a favor: read the story again in its entirety, and then commit to make the time you give to reading this book all about learning the goals we can strive for together as we seek to be Bride Finders for our Master's Son. You can do this. That's not just me saying it. That is God saying it. How do I know? Our Master would only have asked us to do something He knows we can accomplish with His help.

And so my prayer for you as you set out on this journey is...

May your faith be increased. May your heart be flooded with love for those who still need to be welcomed into our Master's family. May doors of opportunity open for you to share our Master's request with others. May you seize every opportunity and be rewarded with yeses for our Master's Son. And may you discover to your own amazement that you are indeed... The Bride Finder.

PREFACE

"*Abraham was now a very old man, and the Lord had blessed him in every way. One day Abraham said to his oldest servant, the man in charge of his household, 'Take an oath by putting your hand under my thigh. Swear by the Lord, the God of heaven and earth, that you will not allow my son to marry one of these local Canaanite women. Go instead to my homeland, to my relatives, and find a wife there for my son Isaac.'*

The servant asked, 'But what if I can't find a young woman who is willing to travel so far from home? Should I then take Isaac there to live among your relatives in the land you came from?' 'No!' Abraham responded. 'Be careful never to take my son there. For the Lord, the God of Heaven, who took me from my father's house and my native land, solemnly promised to give this land to my descendants. He will send his angel ahead of you, and he will see to it that you find a wife there for my son. If she is unwilling to come back with you, then you are free from this oath of mine. But under no circumstances are you to take my son there.'

So the servant took an oath by putting his hand under the thigh of his master, Abraham. He swore to follow Abraham's instructions. Then he loaded ten of Abraham's camels with all kinds of expensive gifts from his master, and he traveled to distant Aram-naharaim. There he went to the town where Abraham's brother Nahor had settled. He made the camels kneel beside a well just outside the town. It was evening, and the women were coming out to draw water.

'O Lord, God of my master, Abraham,' he prayed. 'Please give me success today, and show unfailing love to my master, Abraham. See, I am standing here beside this spring, and the young women of the town are coming out to draw water. This is my request. I will ask one of them, "Please give me a drink from your jug." If she says, "Yes, have a drink, and I will water your camels, too!"—let her

be the one you have selected as Isaac's wife. This is how I will know that you have shown unfailing love to my master.'

Before he had finished praying, he saw a young woman named Rebekah coming out with her water jug on her shoulder. She was the daughter of Bethuel, who was the son of Abraham's brother Nahor and his wife, Milcah. Rebekah was very beautiful and old enough to be married, but she was still a virgin. She went down to the spring, filled her jug, and came up again. Running over to her, the servant said, 'Please give me a little drink of water from your jug.'

'Yes, my Lord,' she answered, 'have a drink.' And she quickly lowered her jug from her shoulder and gave him a drink. When she had given him a drink, she said, 'I'll draw water for your camels, too, until they have had enough to drink.' So she quickly emptied her jug into the watering trough and ran back to the well to draw water for all his camels.

The servant watched her in silence, wondering whether or not the Lord had given him success in his mission. Then at last, when the camels had finished drinking, he took out a gold ring for her nose and two large gold bracelets for her wrists.

'*Whose daughter are you?*' *he asked.* '*And please tell me, would your father have any room to put us up for the night?*'

'*I am the daughter of Bethuel,*' *she replied.* '*My grandparents are Nahor and Milcah. Yes, we have plenty of straw and feed for the camels, and we have room for guests.*'

The man bowed low and worshiped the Lord. '*Praise the Lord, the God of my master, Abraham,*' *he said.* '*The Lord has shown unfailing love and faithfulness to my master, for he has led me straight to my master's relatives.*'

The young woman ran home to tell her family everything that had happened. Now Rebekah had a brother named Laban, who ran out to meet the man at the spring. He had seen the nose-ring and the bracelets on his sister's wrists, and had heard Rebekah tell what the man had said. So he rushed out to the spring, where the man was still standing beside his camels. Laban said to him, '*Come and stay with us, you who are blessed by the Lord! Why are you standing here outside the town when I have a room all ready for you and a place prepared for the camels?*'

So the man went home with Laban, and Laban unloaded the camels, gave him straw for their bedding, fed them, and provided water for the man and the camel drivers to wash their feet. Then food was served. But Abra-

ham's servant said, 'I don't want to eat until I have told you why I have come.'

'All right,' Laban said, 'tell us.'

'I am Abraham's servant,' he explained. 'And the Lord has greatly blessed my master; he has become a wealthy man. The Lord has given him flocks of sheep and goats, herds of cattle, a fortune in silver and gold, and many male and female servants and camels and donkeys.

'When Sarah, my master's wife, was very old, she gave birth to my master's son, and my master has given him everything he owns. And my master made me take an oath. He said, "Do not allow my son to marry one of these local Canaanite women. Go instead to my father's house, to my relatives, and find a wife there for my son."

'But I said to my master, "What if I can't find a young woman who is willing to go back with me?" He responded, "The Lord, in whose presence I have lived, will send his angel with you and will make your mission successful. Yes, you must find a wife for my son from among my relatives, from my father's family. Then you will have fulfilled your obligation. But if you go to my relatives and they refuse to let her go with you, you will be free from my oath."

'So today when I came to the spring, I prayed this prayer: "O Lord, God of my master, Abraham, please give me success on this mission. See, I am standing here beside this spring. This is my request. When a young woman comes to draw water, I will say to her, 'Please give me a little drink of water from your jug.' If she says, 'Yes, have a drink, and I will draw water for your camels, too,' let her be the one you have selected to be the wife of my master's son."

'Before I had finished praying in my heart, I saw Rebekah coming out with her water jug on her shoulder. She went down to the spring and drew water. So I said to her, "Please give me a drink." She quickly lowered her jug from her shoulder and said, "Yes, have a drink, and I will water your camels, too!" So I drank, and then she watered the camels.

'Then I asked, "Whose daughter are you?" She replied, "I am the daughter of Bethuel, and my grandparents are Nahor and Milcah." So I put the ring on her nose, and the bracelets on her wrists.

'Then I bowed low and worshiped the Lord. I praised the Lord, the God of my master, Abraham, because he had led me straight to my master's niece to be his son's wife. So tell me—will you or won't you show unfailing love and *faithfulness to my master? Please tell me yes or no, and then I'll know what to do next.'*

Then Laban and Bethuel replied, 'The Lord has obviously brought you here, so there is nothing we can say. Here is Rebekah; take her and go. Yes, let her be the wife of your master's son, as the Lord has directed.'

When Abraham's servant heard their answer, he bowed down to the ground and worshiped the Lord. Then he brought out silver and gold jewelry and clothing and presented them to Rebekah. He also gave expensive presents to her brother and mother. Then they ate their meal, and the servant and the men with him stayed there overnight.

But early the next morning, Abraham's servant said, 'Send me back to my master.'

'But we want Rebekah to stay with us at least ten days,' her brother and mother said. 'Then she can go.'

But he said, 'Don't delay me. The Lord has made my mission successful; now send me back so I can return to my master.'

'Well,' they said, 'we'll call Rebekah and ask her what she thinks.' So they called Rebekah. 'Are you willing to go with this man?' they asked her.

And she replied, 'Yes, I will go.'

So they said good-bye to Rebekah and sent her away with Abraham's servant and his men. The woman who had been Rebekah's childhood nurse went along with her. They gave her this blessing as she parted:

'Our sister, may you become the mother of many millions!

May your descendants be strong and conquer the cities of their enemies.'

Then Rebekah and her servant girls mounted the camels and followed the man. So Abraham's servant took Rebekah and went on his way.

Meanwhile, Isaac, whose home was in the Negev, had returned from Beer-lahai-roi. One evening as he was walking and meditating in the fields, he looked up and saw the camels coming. When Rebekah looked up and saw Isaac, she quickly dismounted from her camel. 'Who is that man walking through the fields to meet us?' she asked the servant.

And he replied, 'It is my master.' So Rebekah covered her face with her veil. Then the servant told Isaac everything he had done.

And Isaac brought Rebekah into his mother Sarah's tent, and she became his wife. He loved her deeply, and she was a special comfort to him after the death of his mother."

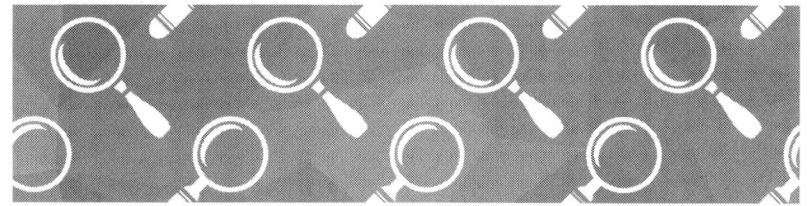

CHAPTER ONE

FOCUS

*"G*o instead to my homeland, to my relatives, and find a wife there for my son Isaac."*
(Genesis 24:4)

One of the funniest— and probably best— compliments I receive after speaking to a group of students is when one of them says, "I really enjoyed your message! I'm ADD too, and I was able to follow you the whole time!" It's always funny to me because I have never been diagnosed with Attention Deficit Disorder or anything related to it. I simply understand that most teenagers can only sit (mostly) still and pay attention about one minute for every year they are old. I've also learned the value of speaking quickly, telling stories, and maintaining high energy while communicating. So for me, it is really less of a personal challenge to overcome and more of a communication device honed over years of experience.

But let's give these young people credit. Some of them may have been wrongfully diagnosed as well. I have heard it said that Gen Z and Gen Alpha are constantly bombarded by so much information that their minds have actually adapted to process information more quickly. It is touted that they determine in eight seconds if a piece of data is important enough to hold onto or jettison as irrelevant. Eight seconds. That might feel like forever if you're trying to win a bull-riding competition, but as someone who communicates for a living, it's frightening to think that I have just eight seconds to hook someone's interest and hopefully keep them engaged for the next 15-30 minutes.

To be fair, I have my own share of struggling to pay attention just as much as the next person. There are mornings when I get up, make coffee, sit down in a quiet room to read the Bible and talk with the Lord privately that my thoughts are all over the place. There is the list of things I know I have to do that day, plus the list of things I didn't get done the day before that now really need to get done. Then there are deeply spiritual thoughts about how massive and magnificent God is, sitting alongside those fairly unimportant thoughts about what I will have for breakfast. Some days it takes almost superhuman effort just to quiet all those thoughts and simply focus.

Whether you realize it or not as a reader, having now written a handful of books, I am learning that it takes intense focus to crank out 20,000-40,000 coherent words which would actually be interesting enough that people would stay tuned after eight seconds, let alone finish reading one of those books. I've heard it from other authors and discovered it to be true for myself: the best writing comes when I stay focused and write consistently every day until I finish a manuscript. But who has time for that when... Hey, hang on a second. I just remembered something else I need to do.

Focus. That's a hard thing to maintain. Whether at work, at home, at the store grocery shopping, or at a church service, it is difficult these days to remain focused. Almost all of us carry a mini-computer in our hands that we call a "phone." I just counted, and I have 162 mobile computing programs called apps currently installed on my "phone." No wonder we are so distracted in our society. Think about it. I just stopped to count all the apps on my phone while I'm writing this book.

The sad truth about this lack of focus is that it robs us of accomplishing so much of eternal value. Because we try to prioritize so many things, keep so many plates spinning, juggle all the areas of life simultaneously, we fail to do the very thing that God declares is the most important task for those of us who know Him, love Him, and follow Him: find a Bride for His Son.

I love that it was just one command. Not 162 apps. One command. It's like God realized we would need some help staying focused. You see, I can focus on one. So can you. And so could Abraham's servant.

In Genesis 24, we read that Abraham laid out an assignment for his servant that involved only one, singular objective: find a wife for his son, Isaac.

Isaac, the son of promise.

Isaac, the son of answered prayers.

Isaac, the son of legacy and descendants to come.

There was only one problem: Isaac didn't have a wife. No wife, no kids. No kids, no grandkids. No grandkids, no "father of many people" for Abraham. God had promised Abraham that he would have many descendants, and yet here was Abraham, old and losing the strength of life, with only one, unmarried son as his hope of that promise coming true. He needed to make sure his son had a bride so that the promises would be fulfilled.

Enter Abraham's servant. This was his oldest and most trusted servant. This man had become a close friend. This man had seen the miracles Abraham had experienced and heard about the times when God showed up to visit Abraham in person. This man knew about the promises.

So it was no surprise to the servant on the day that Abraham called him in for a chat that Abraham felt this urgency to find his son a bride. He may have been surprised that Abraham would choose *him*. He, too, was no spring chicken. But such a prestigious honor... such a daunting responsibility. How could *he* accomplish this task?

One word: Focus.

Abraham didn't complicate the assignment. He asked his servant to do one thing. Just one thing. Go find my son a bride.

Abraham didn't detail exactly *how* the servant should find a bride for his son. He gave him a couple basic parameters, and then essentially said, "Go for it!" He didn't tell the servant whether to take camels or donkeys. He didn't specify that the servant should take gifts, which gifts to take, or how many of each item. Abraham didn't say the servant had to go alone or take others with him. He just gave the servant the assignment and asked him to agree to it.

Did all those things need to be done? Yes. Did decisions have to be made? Yes. But did the servant need to have all that spelled out for him in order to accept the assignment and begin going after it? No.

The request was clear and understandable. He had heard his master's desire, and he knew his master's heart.

He had his focus set before him. He just needed to maintain it.

I'm a big one to talk, though. I get hung up trying to put together one of those boxed pieces of furniture. I'm good at buying the item. I'm good at opening the box. But I begin to slow a little as I take out the plethora of parts. Why do all those bolts have to be different sizes? Then the panic really sets in when I pull out the manual describing how to put the thing together. Seriously, why are there so many pages? I'm used to electronics with a one-page, quick-start guide. And so this is where I usually get bogged down. This is the part where Angela has to step in, remind me to breathe, and start walking me through the steps.

Do you know what has happened to me in those moments? I get so caught up in the steps... in the process... in the details, that I forget to stay focused on the main assignment. All I need to do is remember that my goal is to put together that piece of furniture so that my family has what they need to function in life, and then start at step one.

Before you laugh too hard at my struggles, let me say that I think it is the same kind of struggle which paralyzes many of us as God's servants when it comes to sharing Him with others and inviting them to become a part of His Son's Bride. We get so caught up in the details of who, and where, and why, and when, and how, that we lose focus. That's why this book— and more specifically this chapter— was written: to help us regain our focus.

Our assignment is really quite clear and simple. Before He returned to Heaven, Jesus shared the heart of His Father with His followers by asking them to do one specific thing: find a Bride for the Son.

Mark recorded the request this way: *"Go into all the world and preach the Good News to everyone."* (Mark 16:15). Matthew wrote it with these words: *"...go and make disciples of all the nations..."* (Matthew 28:19). Luke researched and reported the assignment in this light: *"And you will be My witnesses, telling people about Me everywhere...."* (Acts 1:8).

Jesus didn't tell those early disciples how to share Him with others. On that day, He didn't tell them which exact people to talk to about salvation. He just gave them a general idea of where to start, and then He cut them loose to do it.

What happened? They kept their focus, and within two weeks, they had invited 3,000 more people to be the Bride of Christ. Not much more time passed, and they had invited another 2,000 plus people to become the Bride. As they kept their focus, Scripture points out that every day these believers were out sharing Jesus with others and inviting them to be the Bride. And every day, people accepted the invitation. Why? Because the believers didn't lose their focus.

When persecution drove them out of Jerusalem and the surrounding areas, they simply shared Jesus with everyone, everywhere they went. Sure, sometimes the Holy Spirit directed them to or away from certain places, but lots of times they just invited people to be the Bride wherever they ended up next. And everywhere they went, people became a part of the Bride. Why? Because they didn't lose their focus.

So why don't we see more of that today? Believers in some countries still see it happen just like that all the time. Why is it that they continue to find the Bride of

Christ, and often we in our modern, westernized society don't? I believe it is because— in those places— they have determined to stay focused on the one request of the Master: find My Son a Bride.

Too often, we get distracted. We lose focus. We see a shiny object. We hear a tempting voice. Or less noticeably, we simply allow ourselves to get overwhelmed by all the steps that might be involved, and we forget the one, main, overall objective: find a Bride for the Master's Son.

At one church where we have had the privilege of serving, I had a team member call me to discuss an outreach effort the church was going to pursue. We had set a date. We had identified reaching the lost and unchurched as our goal. I had shared a general theme for the day that I believe the Lord had laid on my heart. And then I cut the team loose to go for it. When they came back to me with some of the details for the day, there had been some concern over certain details of the plan. What we realized in that moment was that we started to lose focus on the purpose of the day. We had gotten so deep in the weeds and so caught up in all the steps that we almost forgot that the focus of the whole day was to reach lost people who could be invited to become a part of Christ's Bride.

Can I encourage you today? You don't have to have it all figured out to get started obeying. You don't have to know exactly what you will say when the moment arises. You don't have to know exactly where every interaction with a potential Bride might take place. In the words of Angela when we are putting together one of those pieces of furniture with all the parts and the epic manual, "Take a deep breath. You can do this."

You can, you know. You can do this. I can do this. We can all do this. Think about it: the Master chose *you*. He has asked *you* to find a Bride for His Son. He didn't make a mistake. He knows you and you know Him. He knows you love Him. He knows you want to please Him. He trusts you. He knows your limitations. He knows your concerns. Still, He chose you. And since He chose you, then He knows you can do this. Otherwise, He would not have asked you to do it.

I know there can be moments when we tense up, and it seems like we can't even remember our own name—

like when I'm trying to order at the fast food restaurant drive-thru and they ask if the order is correct, but I didn't understand a word they said— let alone how to share Jesus with someone. I get it. No, really, I do.

Recently, I stepped up to preach in the Sunday morning service at our church. I was wrapping up a series of five messages, and the message that day was the culmination of them all. It was to be compounded interest from all the messages. This was going to be the walk-off, grand-slam-homer in the bottom of the ninth that changed every listener's life going forward. (At least it felt that way in my mind.) The only problem was that I forgot to charge the iPad from which I normally access my notes as I preach. So I plugged its charger into the wall on the side of the church during the worship portion of the service. It charged to 19%, which was going to be just enough for me to make it through the message.

I stepped to the platform, led us through a time of transitioning from worship and prayer into the portion of the service designed for the Word of God to be shared. Then I tapped on the iPad, brought it to life, opened the Pages app where my notes were supposed to be, and tapped on the document containing my message notes only to find that it would not open the document because the notes were not there.

You see, earlier that week I had been blessed to come across a crazy-great deal on a Macbook Pro laptop from a friend-of-a-friend on Facebook Marketplace, and I had typed the message for that Sunday on the laptop. I had set up everything between all my devices to sync up so that I could access each item from any of them. That meant I should have been able to type the message on the laptop and open it to preach from on the iPad. But it wasn't working.

I tried opening the document on my phone, only to find that the font size was so small on the phone screen that I couldn't read it well enough to preach from while wearing my contacts. I tried the iPad again... all while people watched ever so patiently and waited for me to share something meaningful to their lives from God's Word.

Finally, in a moment of panic, I had to ask Angela to go to my office there at the church and get the laptop. She must have seen the panic in my eyes because she jumped up and went after it. In that moment, I was just hoping that all was not lost on it as well because I got so distracted that I could literally only remember one word from the message. I couldn't remember the opening story that I had hoped would grab everyone's attention— even the Gen Z'ers in the crowd with whom I only had eight seconds. I couldn't remember the points. I couldn't remember the two verses of Scripture from which we had been studying in-depth for the past month. I couldn't recall any illustrations. I only remembered one word and that I was going to have a man in the crowd help me do a demonstration that day.

I had locked up. I was frozen. I was seriously concerned that I would not be able to do what I was supposed to do in that moment. That had never happened to me before, and I wasn't sure we were going to be able to get through the message successfully that morning.

Angela came back quickly with the laptop, I opened it, clicked on the program, and it wouldn't open. More panic. More trying to explain and apologize to everyone sitting in the audience staring at me. Finally it opened, and I was able to open the document with the message in it.

Something interesting happened though, in that moment. I took one look at my notes, and suddenly, it all came flooding back. That one reminder got me kick-started, and I knew everything was going to be all right. (I don't know that the message was as epic as I had originally envisioned after all that, but the Lord still worked in people's lives despite my technological hiccup.)

Maybe you've had a moment of panic in your life before when it came time to share Jesus with someone, and you just froze. Maybe you're still frozen. Don't worry. There's just one thing you need to remember to get started: Your assignment is to find a Bride for the Master's Son. Stay focused. You don't have to have all the details at this moment. You just need to get started. Start, and God will help you succeed.

Over the next seven chapters, we will learn some more lessons from Abraham's servant that will help us find the Bride for our Master's Son. But for now, let's just remember to focus on *this* being our goal while we still live on this planet. It's just one assignment. And as we focus on that one assignment, the Holy Spirit will help us with all the other steps along the way.

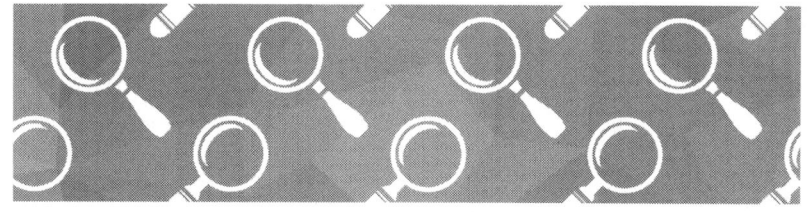

CHAPTER TWO

IT'S NOT ABOUT ME

"'I *am Abraham's servant,' he explained."*
(Genesis 24:34)

Moment of transparency...

I'm not great with people's names. Even when I'm at an event, and they make us all wear those stick-on little rectangular "Hello, my name is" name-tags, I still forget

17

people's names. I know. That's really not good for someone whose whole life is about loving and ministering to
people.

Names are important. Knowing someone's name matters. People like to be known and acknowledged. I remember discovering the power of people's names one
weekend when I was invited to speak at a retreat for a
youth group. My youth pastor friend had invited me to
come challenge his students, and I was excited for the
opportunity. I showed up at the state park where they
were holding the retreat, hung out with everyone, and
then we all headed down to this large dock situated on
a pristine lake. As the sun began to drop in the early
evening sky, we worshiped, and my friend introduced me
as I came to share the word God had put on my heart for
those students. I just knew it was for a number of them
there, though I didn't know exactly who.

I came to the end of the message, and as I do at the
end of every message— because I'm a preacher and don't
just "give talks"— I gave the opportunity for people to
respond to what God was saying. I was so disappointed
when only a few students responded because I knew in
my heart that this truth was for more of that group.

Determined to leave that between God and those who either did or didn't respond, I led those responding in a time of prayer. Then I invited my friend to come back and wrap up the service.

He stepped up and told the guy on the acoustic guitar to keep playing because he felt like there were more students who should have responded. He began calling out names and saying, "So-and-so, this is what you and I just talked about last week. I know God was speaking to you tonight in that message." He proceeded to name five to seven more students out of the group of more than fifty who were sitting on that dock. After speaking those names and talking about how he knew that message was for them, he gave the opportunity for people to respond again to the message I had preached. I was blown away by how many of the group responded that time. We prayed with the students responding, and the service ended.

Later he and I talked about why that happened, and I learned something at that retreat that weekend. I had supposed that maybe I had just not connected, or that he knew something I didn't. But that wasn't really it at all.

He told me how— as their group had grown beyond 100 students and was on its way to 200 each week— he was struggling to get to know the newer students who came, and he wanted to at least learn their names. So he had taught his students to bring any friend they brought to the youth service over to meet him before they started and introduce their friend by name. As he talked with the friend, he would try to say their name four or five times casually in the conversation in order to lock it in his mind. And then, during his message in the youth service that night, he would try to say the name of every new student he had met to further lock their names in his mind and to let them know that he knew they were there.

He then told me how he began to notice something unique happening. Whenever he would say these new students' names in the message, they would respond to the message at the end when the opportunity was given. It so caught his attention that he began to test it out with regular students. To his surprise, again every student whose name he called while he preached began to respond at the end of those messages.

Then it hit him. It was because, when he said their name, it made the message personal to them. Students love to be seen, noticed, recognized, and acknowledged. They're not all vain. They just want to be known.

Teenagers want you to know their name. When I was serving as state youth director for our fellowship in another state, students I met at one event would see me at another event later that year, or maybe the same event a year later, and when they saw me again, the first thing they would ask me was if I remembered their name.

Teenagers aren't wrong for wanting someone to know their name. For many kids, they feel overlooked and insignificant because they are not adults yet. People make them feel like they are not as valuable sometimes. In some ways, part of the adolescent years is becoming known and recognized.

Sadly, the society in which we live in the western world has often pampered and reinforced that sentiment far into adulthood, not ever reaching the place where people can be comfortable enough in their own skin that they don't feel compelled to make sure people know their name.

In fact, our world has become obsessed with people knowing our name. We want brand recognition for our names. Our culture says to make sure people know your name... the name of your YouTube channel... your Instagram handle. It's as if our world says, "If no one knows your name, then you don't matter."

I understand the feeling all too well as an author. The very fact that I write books means that I want someone to read them. That means people have to know they exist. And I am the primary cheerleader for those books, which means people have to at least know about me in the process.

When I wrote my first book, I had a dream that some friend of a friend of a friend would hand my book to a major Christian publisher, and I would become a household name. The way it actually played out was that, after a year or so, I was just glad to have sold enough books to cover the money I had paid others to edit the rough draft and design the cover. The second book I wrote paid for itself a little more quickly, but copies still weren't flying off Amazon's printing press. And still, no big-time publisher was offering to make me a New York Times #1 best seller.

So, I began to research how to get my books out there and impacting the lives of many people. The problem was, everything I found in my research basically said,

"Promote yourself, promote yourself, promote your-self." It was all about making a big social media splash, offering one thing to people for free so that you could get their email address and send them offers to sign up for your $1,000 masterclass, getting influencers to talk about you, being on as many podcasts as possible so you can get your name out there, and asking your friends to talk you up as well. The gist was to make yourself known so that you could sell books.

And yet, that isn't the culture of Heaven. Heaven is only concerned that the name of our Master and His Son are made known. There is a reason that this should be okay with us, and I'll get to that in a minute. Yet as those who are to be finding a bride for the Son, it isn't our priority or responsibility to make sure people know who we are, but rather who we represent.

By the time I finished my third book and was ready to publish it, I had decided I wasn't going the route the world told me to go. I might not sell as many books because I am not "known," but it wasn't about me in the first place. It's about getting out a message that changed my life. It's about helping others experience God in an amazing way and know Him more intimately.

Sure, I'm proud of the books the Lord helps me write. It's a dream that was a long time coming about in my life, and it's a dream many people have but never fulfill. And yet, writing books isn't about me. It never has been, even though I thought for a while that's what I would have to make it about in order for my writing to be a success. Now I realize that the best approach I can take is to simply help people get to know My Master, whether they ever learn my name or not.

I don't know if you caught this when you read the account we're studying in this book, but Abraham's servant was basically the only person in the whole story not named. Yet he appears to be the main character. Sixty-seven verses, and there was not one mention of his name. He is involved in every verse except the very first and the very last verses. Yet, he remains un-named. Even when he was asked outright about who he was and why he had arrived in that distant land, he simply introduced himself by saying, "I am Abraham's servant." It's okay... because it wasn't about him.

I love that. That kind of humility is rare. But that kind of commitment to the cause rather than his own name is almost inconceivable in our world today. And yet...

that's what it is going to take for us to be effective Bride finders.

You see, it's not about me. It's not about you. It's not about anyone except our Master, His Son, and the Bride He longs to have by His side. Winning people to Jesus— finding Him a Bride— isn't about introducing them to *us* and getting them to fall in love with *us*. It's about connecting them to *Him*. It's about telling who our Master is and why He sent us on this mission. It's about letting them know all about the blessings that await them if they accept His offer. It's about Him knowing *their* name. It's about *them* falling in love with *Him*.

So what if everyone else's name gets mentioned in the story of your life except yours? So what if you seem hidden in the very story where you are intricately involved? "So what?" you might ask. "How can you be so harsh, Allen? Don't I matter?"

Of course you do. And I told you that I would tell you why it doesn't matter whether our names are known or not. So here's the little secret the servant held onto that we need to hold onto as well: His master knew his name.

You see, just because I said that the servant's name wasn't mentioned doesn't mean he didn't have a name.

He had a name. And his master knew that name. In fact, he knew it well. He picked *that* servant on purpose because he was Abraham's oldest and most trusted servant. That means he had been in relationship with Abraham a long time. That means they knew each other well. Abraham would not have entrusted such a special assignment to just anyone. This mattered too much. There was too much at stake, too much on the line. So he called for *THAT* servant. In other words, the master knew the servant's name... even if no one else did. The son knew the servant's name... even if no one else did.

And though the writer of Genesis didn't share his name with us, it's okay. The master's name was shared. The son's name was shared. The bride-to-be's name was shared. Even her family members' names were shared. And not once did the servant rise up to say, "Hey, somebody be sure to write my name down in this story."

Why? Because the story wasn't about him. Oh sure, he played a pivotal role in it all, and I'm sure he was commended by Abraham for succeeding. In fact, his stature probably grew in Abraham's estimation, and he knew he had chosen the right guy for the job.

Beyond Abraham knowing who he was, the servant knew who he was himself. He knew he was the choice servant of his master, the one hand-picked for this mission. He knew where he stood with Abraham. As for anyone else knowing who he was, they only needed to know who he came on behalf of and what his mission was. He didn't need to be known, famous, or recognized. He just needed to succeed at his mission.

Here's the thing... this whole finding a Bride for Christ isn't really about us. It's about our Master and His Son. It's about loving our Lord so much that we would gladly do whatever He asks of us in order to advance His Kingdom and grow His family. It's about a willingness to make *His* name known...whether ours ever is or not.

So don't fret today if you're not a world famous YouTuber or TikToker. Don't worry that you follow one hundred times the number of people who follow you on social media. Remember that it's not about whether or not they learn *your* name. It only matters that they know His name. Make it your goal to make Him known... to make Him famous... and you will be on your way to being an amazing Bride finder!

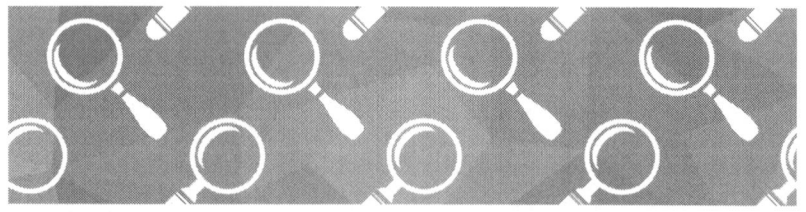

CHAPTER THREE

NEVER HURTS TO ASK

"'O Lord, God of my master, Abraham,' he prayed. 'Please give me success today, and show unfailing love to my master, Abraham... This is my request... This is how I will know that You have shown unfailing love to my master.'" (Genesis 24:12-14)

I *love* getting a great deal on something I'm buying. Whether I'm at a garage sale, a restaurant, a car dealership, or a real estate office, I'm probably going to ask for a discount. It's not that I'm a cheapskate. I just hate having to pay more for something than necessary. Plus, sometimes it is just fun to see how great a deal I can get. I don't mind the seller making *some* money off me. I just don't want them to make *all* their money off me. And I'm just bold enough to ask if I can get it for less.

If I'm going to buy something on Facebook Marketplace, you can be pretty certain that I'm going to ask if they would take a little bit less than what they are asking for the item. Take the used Macbook Pro I'm writing this book on for example. The person was asking $350, and I had already decided to ask them if they would take $300. When I asked if it was available, they told me someone was supposed to be getting it that evening. I asked them to let me know if that person didn't show or didn't end up wanting it. A few hours later, I got a message back from them that it was available if I still wanted it, but they wouldn't take a dollar less than $230. After re-reading it several times to make sure I had not transposed the numbers in my mind, I gladly accepted and went to buy it that afternoon. That time I didn't have to ask them to take less, but I was ready to ask.

When it comes to buying a car, we all realize the price listed is never the actual price that will be paid. It just isn't. I know it. The salesman knows it. His sales manager knows it. In the end, they want to know what it's going to take to get me in that baby today. In the end, I want to know that they had to give me more for my trade-in and took less for their vehicle. Even though the last vehicle we bought came from one of those online car dealers where "the price you see is the price you pay," they actually offered us more for our vehicle and already had a lower-priced vehicle than others. So guess who I bought from without blinking an eye? I get it honestly. Back in the day, my grandpa would work a whole car deal, and then to top it off would make them agree to fill the tank up with gas or the deal was a bust. Man, I miss that guy. Heroes are made of that stuff. So I ask.

If I'm buying a house, you can take to the bank the fact that I'm going to ask my realtor to see if the seller would take less, or at least give us something extra to sweeten the deal. I've learned after a few times buying and selling houses that there are several places across the purchase to score a little deal. It's not just about how much they will come off the original asking price. There can be negotiations after the inspection. If the house doesn't appraise at the agreed-upon price, there is more room to dicker and come away with a sweeter deal. Some people will even ask for money toward closing costs. Hey, I figure if it lowers my house note every month, I'm for it. So I ask.

I often joke with a cashier or waitress as I'm paying by asking them if I can get "the good-lookin' guy discount." Angela and the boys sometimes roll their eyes. The cashier will sometimes laugh. Or sometimes they just stare at me like they don't understand. (I try to not to be insulted when they stare.) Sometimes they are quick-witted enough to reply, "Ohhhh, sorry, that was yesterday. You just missed it." But you can bet that I don't mind taking a discount if they take me up on it—even if it is just to humor my attempt. If they offer the discount, I'm going to try to get it. Like the time we were in Ross on the day of the week when they give senior citizens a discount on all their purchases, and the cashier asked me if I would like the discount. I don't know why she asked. I was dressed more like a youngster that day than most. Maybe she saw that hint of gray in my sideburns that is slowly creeping toward my temples. But not willing to miss out on a good deal, I asked what the age cut-off was, and she replied, "Fifty-five years old." I told her that I was sorry, but that I wouldn't qualify for that discount for a few more years. She smiled, shrugged, and said, "Well, I'll give it to you anyway." What can I say? Favor ain't fair, baby. Yes, you know I took the deal.

The truth is, it's not that I can't afford what I'm buying. I wouldn't be buying it if I couldn't afford it. I suppose I could try to sound super spiritual and tell you that I try to get a discount because I am trying to be a good steward of God's resources. And I do want to steward well what He entrusts into my care. But quite honestly, sometimes it's just fun to see if I can get a better deal on something. And the more deals I get, the more fun the challenge becomes on the next purchase. So, you might be wondering, "If it's not about the money, then why ask? Why go to all the trouble?"

I ask for one reason and one reason only: Why not?

Some people are so afraid of asking. They are more worried about what someone will think of them than they are interested in saving twenty percent. They would be embarrassed to ask someone to take less than the price on the tag. They are more concerned that the person ringing up their sale will think that they are somehow impoverished— or some kind of cheapskate from one of those reality TV shows— and they think that would somehow make them less valuable as a person.

Others fear getting turned down — as if being told "no" were going to somehow irreparably damage their psyche. I'm just bold enough to not worry about what they are thinking of me. I figure the worst they can say is, "No." Think about this, though: Even if they don't give me all of what I'm asking for, maybe they will meet me part-way. If they do, I've saved a little that I can use for something else... something else which I can hopefully get a deal on as well. And then I have another great story to tell about how God has blessed my life in some way.

Again, why not?

James, the Lord's half-brother, who was one of the early leaders of the New Testament Church, wrote a letter to believers and said that often the reason we don't "have" is simple: We don't ask. Do you know why many people don't get the discounts I get? It's not because I have some magical quality— although God certainly bestows favor on my life, in my opinion. And before you suggest it, there is no "good looking guy discount." (I made that one up on my own.) I receive the discounts I receive for one simple reason: because I ask for the discount. Pure and simple, I receive because I ask.

So I totally resonate with Abraham's servant when he asks God to make his mission successful. Could he have just obeyed Abraham and gone on the mission? Sure, but he asks God anyway. Is it possible that he would still have found a wife for Isaac without asking? Maybe. Then why ask God for help? I say, "Why not ask?"

Abraham's servant had been with Abraham a long time. He had watched God shower his master with favor. Abraham didn't always deserve the goodness God showed him. Abraham had made his fair share of mistakes. But Abraham kept going back to God and looking for His help. Take, for instance, the time when God told Abraham that He was going to destroy Sodom and Gomorrah because of their wickedness and Abraham asked God not to destroy them because his nephew Lot had moved to live near those cities. He asked God if He would spare the cities if one hundred righteous people could be found in them. God agreed. Abraham negotiated a little more and asked if God would spare them for fifty righteous people living there. God agreed. Abraham took it down to ten righteous people. God agreed. Finally, Abraham threw out the lowball offer and asked God to spare the entire cities if even ONE righteous person could be found living there. Guess what God did in response to Abraham's outlandish request? He said yes to it. Turned out, even Lot and his family weren't righteous, and God had to destroy both cities. But God did something amazing. He rescued Lot and his family because Abraham had asked.

That's the kind of environment this servant had lived in for many years. Now it was his turn to be involved with a significant effort. His master was counting on him. It was all riding on him. Or was it? I believe he realized something we all need to realize if we are going to be effective Bride finders: All of the burden for success doesn't have to rest squarely on our shoulders. We can ask God for help. In fact, we should ask God for help.

God wants us to ask Him for help. And that is exactly what the servant does. He asks God to bless his efforts, and he does it in four ways...

First, he asks God for something successful. He doesn't dilly-dally around and kind of, sort of, almost ask God to help him a little bit. He asks God for success. He's not playing to not lose; he's playing to win. He doesn't want just anyone. He doesn't want to bring home some young lady that could be, possibly might be "the one." He wants to come out of this mission knowing that he succeeded in doing exactly what was asked of him by his master. So he prayed for God to give him success. Not make him work for it. Give him success.

Too often, we just go out there on our own, trying to accomplish the mission in our own power and ability. We come up with our own ideas. We determine who we will attempt to win to the Lord. Instead, we should take a little screenshot from the playbook of Abraham's servant and ask God to give us success. To ask for His help might be a little humbling, but that's probably not such a bad thing. And while we are asking, let's ask big. Let's ask for success. Let's ask God to help the soup kitchen impact lives so powerfully that they become part of the Bride of Christ. Let's ask God to help our creatively designed, Christian-themed t-shirts to sell like crazy so that more people read them and have their hearts opened to hearing more about the Lord. Let's ask God to help us have conversations with family members or friends at the holidays that will turn into eternity-transforming moments. Let's ask God for success. And I believe that when we ask, we will receive because those prayers are prayers that line up with the heart of the One who wants a Bride for His Son even more than we do.

Second, he asks God for something certain. He acknowledges what he has seen of God: that God shows unfailing love to those who follow and obey Him. Over the years, this servant watched God love Abraham and Sarah... Isaac... Hagar and Ishmael... and even Lot's dysfunctional family. None were ever perfect, but God just kept sticking with them, loving them despite all their faults and flaws. He realized that the nature of God is unconditional love for people; unconditional love that never stops. That must have made some kind of impact on this man because when he asks God to show up and help, he asks God to one more time show up with that unfailing love for his master Abraham.

The servant asks for that one characteristic out of all God's attributes. That's significant. It isn't about how good Abraham is. It isn't about how faithful Abraham has been. It's about how good God is and about how faithful God is. He asks God to show up and reveal that characteristic once more to his master. And because he is submitted to his master— doing his master's bidding— he believes that will trickle down to him on this mission.

Sometimes people don't share their faith with others and invite them to come to know Jesus because they haven't always lived the kind of life they think they would have to in order for God to use them. Yet God looks at the heart. None of us are perfect. It is His unfailing love which reached out to us and saved us. It is His kindness which leads to repentance. We didn't deserve His kindness and love. And that is a good thing to keep in mind, because the people we are going to invite to be a part of the Bride of Christ are going to need to know that unfailing love for themselves. They need to hear our story of how God has faithfully loved us even when we weren't quite as faithful as we should have been. A great, heart-felt prayer goes something like this, "God, I may not deserve it, but please show Yourself to be who You are to me and the person I'm about to share You with despite my imperfections and theirs." That is a prayer God loves to answer.

Third, he asks God for something specific. The servant asked God to "Let her say 'yes' when I ask for a drink of water from her jug." While hospitality to strangers was common in that day, he was asking for an open door. Nothing wrong with that request. We should always ask God for favor when we are going to share Him with others. We can ask Him for the conversation to turn a certain way and open the door for us to share Him with that person. We can ask Him to soften their heart and prepare them to really hear what we say. We can ask Him to help them open up to us personally so that we have the opportunity to invite them into a relationship with Jesus. Those are specific prayers God will answer.

And then fourth, he asks God for something extraordinary. He requests of God, "Let her also say that she will water my camels as well." This would have been a confirming sign. It's one thing to give a stranger a cup of water. It's another thing to lower your jug into the deep well, pull up the now-full, heavy jug of said water by hand, dump it into a trough for the camels to start drinking... and then do it about 299 more times because that's about how many times it would have taken to water the camels the servant brought. In case you didn't know, camels drink an astronomical amount of water. It's like thirty gallons each. And there were ten camels. Do the math.

So when the servant asks God to let the sign which confirms he is on the right track about who to invite to marry his master's son be that she would offer to take on this ridiculous task, he knew he was asking for the extraordinary. He was asking for the miraculous. He was asking that God would mark that moment with such power that someone who didn't know him, his master, or his master's son would on their own offer to do something so uncommon that the servant could make no mistake that this was going to be a marriage made in Heaven.

It's not wrong to ask God to help us know that He's with us... that He's helping us... that He is working on our behalf when we want to invite someone to be a part of His family. He is the God of the extraordinary. He is the God of the miraculous. Just read Scripture. How many supernatural acts does it take for us to realize that God knows how to do stuff we can't do? Maybe you're so nervous about sharing Jesus with someone that you need a little reassurance. Take a note from the servant: God doesn't get mad when we ask Him to do the extraordinary. That's because it's not extraordinary for Him; it just is for us. For Him, it's a walk in the park, a cake walk, or any other kind of walk captured in colloquial sayings. In other words, our extraordinary request is easy-peasy, lemon-squeezy for Him.

"So you need some reassurance that I'm helping you introduce someone I love to My Son? Oh, you think that would be too difficult? Okay, let's just see about that! Boom! Extraordinary request delivered. Now let's go get 'em!"

You can't out-ask God. Jesus Himself said that we should *ask*, and it will be given to us. He told a story about a widow asking an unjust judge to help her in order to help us understand that it is okay to *ask* our loving Heavenly Father for help. He said we could agree together in *asking*, and that God would respond. He said we could *ask* anything in His Name— that is, according to His will and in line with who He is— and God would do it. Is there anything more in line with God's heart than people being brought into His family? I don't believe so. His Word says in 2 Peter 3:9 that He is not willing that *any* should perish, but that *all* should come to repentance. So it just makes sense that we should *ask* Him to help us as we invite them to be the Bride.

When it comes to inviting people to join God's family, we should ask God to show His unfailing love in the process. We should ask Him to save specific people... at specific times... in specific ways. And we should ask Him to confirm that we are working in line with His will by making it all come together. Why? Because it never hurts to ask.

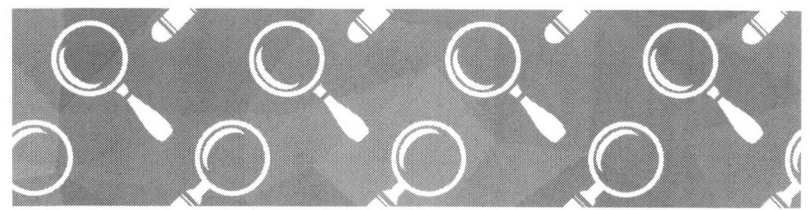

CHAPTER FOUR

GIVE

" Then at last, when the camels had finished drinking, he took out a gold ring for her nose and two large gold bracelets for her wrists." (Genesis 24:22)

Rowland Howard originally penned the lyric, "For you never miss the water till the well runs dry." It's about appreciation, and I didn't get that as a kid. I would complain about having to eat leftovers or leave much of said leftover food on my plate, and after supper head to the trashcan to throw away any scraps still laying on the stoneware circle in my hand. Like all good parents, mine would tell me not to complain about leftovers because they were perfectly good. When I would express my displeasure, they would feed me the line many a parent has fed their kids. Go ahead and recite it with me if you've ever heard it: "There are starving children around the world who would love to have those leftovers you are about to throw away."

Now, I was neither bold— nor stupid— enough to say out loud the smart-aleck thoughts that were going through my mind like, "Well, let's box it up and send it to them then because I don't want any more of it." Good thing. I probably survived in life to be this age because of that infinitesimal wisdom that somehow made its way into my immature cranium.

My problem was, of course, that I had no sense of appreciation at the time. I didn't get how much that food had cost to purchase. I didn't realize how much time it took to cook it. I didn't understand the complexities of trying to please five different sets of tastebuds. I didn't have any sense of what amounted to nutritional value in various foods or why that would matter to my personal health. Nor did I comprehend how serious and real the malnutrition epidemic actually was throughout our nation— let alone third-world countries across the planet.

Obviously, as I have aged— and hopefully matured some— I have come to have a better grasp on how special it is to be able to go to the pantry, or the fridge, or the freezer and choose what food we want to eat. I get that some people around the world are grateful for the beans and rice that someone can provide for them every day at an outreach mission. My brother-in-law and sister served in rural communities in the heart of our nation where the lack of food in families' homes they described to me is almost unbelievable. I have seen the soup kitchen at our church serve the undernourished elderly and homeless in our community first-hand. So if my kids get tired of hearing something from me as they grow up, it probably isn't that line about leftovers for the starving kids around the world, but that I thank God almost every night as we pray together as a family that we had food to eat that day... and clothes to wear... and a roof over our heads... and clean bottled water to drink. Thing is, I mean it from the depths of my heart. I realize now what I didn't grasp then: God is generous. He is far more generous with us than we typically comprehend.

More importantly as it relates to our mission, it is His generosity which should encourage us to be generous as we reach out to others and invite them to be the Bride of Christ. The Lord has been amazingly generous toward us. He is generous with His love. He is extremely generous with His mercy and grace. He is generous with His protection and power. Day-in-and-day-out, our Master is generous with us. Not only has He saved us and made us His own, but He feeds us... clothes us... guides us... encourages us... lifts us up... and gives us purpose. He is generous. It is His heart. It is His character. It is His very nature. He has not withheld any good thing from us.

In our story, the servant worships the Lord— giving praise freely— and is generous with others whenever the Lord brings a part of the assignment together for him. Why? He has a heart of gratitude. He is grateful to God, and he is grateful to his master for entrusting this task of monumental consequence into his care. Plus, he realizes that it is his master's wealth he is sharing, not his own. He loses nothing by being generous. No limits were set by Abraham as to how generous the servant could be. He wanted to represent his master well, and generosity spoke to the heart of his master. He gave freely and richly to Rebekah and to her family. He wanted them to know they were valued. He wanted them to know all that his master had to offer.

Generosity still speaks to the heart of our Master today as well. A heart of selfishness never drew anyone toward the Lord. This is because stinginess and selfishness don't resemble our Master in any way. As His representatives, He wants us to show the same generosity to others which He has shown to us. He has plenty of love to share. He has plenty of grace to give. He has plenty of healing, provision, and hope to pour out on everyone who needs it. The truth is, He also has plenty of money, food, clothing, and any other physical items people might need. He is well-able to provide anything that is needed to draw the lost to His heart.

Not only is God able, but He is willing to share His wealth with those to whom He is reaching out to in our world. Get this: He's willing to give it even before they become a part of His family. Many times in the Gospels, we read of Jesus healing, or feeding, or resurrecting someone who had not yet committed to follow Him. In fact, almost nowhere in the Gospels do we hear whether or not most of those He worked miracles for followed Him at all. One was a Jewish synagogue leader. Another was a Roman officer. Nothing in Scripture says whether or not these types of people committed their lives to following Christ. Yet He gave freely and abundantly to them in hopes that they would turn their hearts toward His.

So it stands to reason that if we are ever going to be effective at reaching the lost and seeing them become a part of the Bride of Christ, we must also be generous. We must be generous in recognizing how much He has done for us. We should always be grateful to the Lord for saving us and welcoming us into His forever family. If we ever forget how special that gift of mercy and grace is, then we will care little whether or not others get to experience it. And we must also be generous in our interactions with those we are hoping to reach for Christ.

GENEROUS IN ATTITUDE

When it comes to reaching others for Him, if we have any hope that they will receive our Master's invitation to be a part of the Bride for His Son, we must begin by being generous in our attitudes. If we are looking down our noses at "those lost people," they are not going to be inclined to want to hear the invitation we offer. People can tell if we are genuinely interested in them or if we simply want another notch on our spiritual gun. People can tell the difference between someone who truly loves them and someone who despises them but feels a guilty need to help "the less fortunate."

Recently, a Christian man from a local business contacted our church about the soup kitchen our church operates each Thursday to feed the undernourished in our community. He wanted to see the soup kitchen in action and possibly serve. And he wanted to know if it would be okay to bring along a gentleman who handles their social media to do a story about the soup kitchen. Obviously, we are always grateful for help and for a little free publicity. So we said yes. I was running late getting over to the other building where the soup kitchen operates on that particular Thursday because of some other ministry responsibilities, and so this gentleman and his social media guy had been there about thirty minutes when I arrived. I asked him if they had met everyone and what they thought about it all. His response was amazement. He told me how he had been around numerous churches and church people over the years, but what stood out to him about the group serving in the soup kitchen that day was their authenticity and humility. He— and his social media helper— went on and on about how they just couldn't get past that no one cared about acknowledgement or recognition. They just wanted to serve and bless people in need. He couldn't remember the last time he had seen believers truly serve with that kind of selfless, loving attitude. We shot a video for his business to use about their time with the soup kitchen that day, but interestingly, he didn't air it for a week or two. And before he did, his business sent a check to help cover all the food needed to feed the hungry in our area for at least one Thursday.

What was it that stood out to him? The attitude of those in the church serving the lost. No arrogance. No thinking less of those we are serving. Just a genuine love and desire to meet people's needs. What he didn't realize is that when we launched the soup kitchen, we determined that it would never be about trying to get people to come to the church. We just wanted them to know God loves them and would meet their needs. But now ten months into the journey to serve our community, two individuals from the soup kitchen have made the church their own. Why? I believe it was due in large part to the attitude of those who serve in the soup kitchen.

GENEROUS IN SPEECH

We must also be generous in the way we speak with people. The servant showed great respect for Rebekah and her family. He used requests instead of demands. He honored their requests with gracious words. He asked her if she would give him a drink of water. That interaction reminds me so very much of the interaction between Jesus and the woman at the well in Samaria. Neither demanded or talked down to the lady with whom they spoke. Instead, they were generous with kind speech.

I spent a decade working for a leader who seemed to be the king of generous speech. He seemed to always have the right words for every occasion and for every person. Whether on a hospital visit, in a business meeting, having lunch in a restaurant, or at a funeral, he just always had the best... most perfectly fitting... generously gracious words to speak to someone. He knew how to make every person in his presence feel as if they were important and valued.

I remember one time when he told me that a pastor had asked his permission to talk to me about leaving my role and coming to serve at their church. My boss said, "I told that pastor, 'Absolutely not. We love him around here and don't want him going anywhere.'" I would have done almost anything for my boss.

And even though he was my boss and could have ordered me to do whatever task he wanted done, he always asked if I would do them. I saw him do it countless times with my other co-workers too. He was the epitome of a godly gentleman. I say "godly" because God isn't the kind who is harsh and demanding, and my boss reminded me of how God treats people. I learned so many great lessons from that leader, but I am still working to attain his level of generous speech.

I've tried to learn to cultivate this generosity of speech over the years as a preacher. It's so easy to categorize and generalize people and situations. It's so easy to "call a spade a spade," and act like people just need to toughen up to hear the truth. But Scripture doesn't just say that we are to speak truth. The Apostle Paul— who interestingly enough did not think of himself as a great orator— wrote in Ephesians 4:15 that "...[we are to] speak the truth in love, growing in every way more and more like Christ..."

Our efforts to draw people to Jesus should be framed in language full of love and kindness. For Scripture also says that it is God's kindness which draws, or leads, people to repentance (Romans 2:4). So I've discovered that I can say things in a way which is generous with love, kindness, hope, and encouragement, and still invite people to give up their old life to begin a new one as the Bride for my Master's Son.

A little generosity of speech goes a long way.

GENEROUS IN ACTION

And then finally, we must be generous in our actions toward people. When I say actions, maybe I should be a little more clear: I mean we should give something that costs us. Over the past few decades, I have consistently encouraged people who want to reach the lost to give financially to the cause of inviting the lost to know the Son and become His Bride. That usually means giving to missions and outreach efforts. Why give financially? Because we know that Jesus— the One for whom we are trying to gain a Bride— said in Matthew 6:21, "Wherever your treasure is, there the desires of your heart will also be." So it makes sense that the more we invest in reaching the lost, the more the potential Bride-to-be will have a place in our heart. And the more the lost have a place in our heart, the more likely we are to try to win them over to come meet the Son with us.

Giving to some of the lost in this world almost always helps us open up to reach more of the lost in the world. Practically every person I have ever taken on a missions trip finds it hard to get or cut loose of the funds to travel half-way around the world to reach the lost. But then something unexpected happens in their heart. They meet the lost people in that location we are going to reach. And as the week to ten days we are there rolls along, they begin to care deeply for those people. They see their needs and want to meet them. They end up loving those people and wanting to be generous to them. They want to give them all the cash they brought with them. They want to give them any snacks they have left in their luggage. They want to give them their good clothes or shoes so that these people they have come to love don't have to wear their tattered clothes or go shoeless any longer. They will leave instruments that they never would have parted with back home with these people they now love . They are willing to buy items like generators that cost hundreds or thousands of dollars so that the missionary can reach more of the lost who now have a place in their heart. They want to give all they can.

But something else interesting almost always happens on those trips: they begin to think about all the lost people back home where they live and about what they could do to be generous to those lost... what they could do to reach out to them. They realize the person across the street or across town who is lost could also be the potential Bride of Christ. Generally, they now can hardly wait to go on the next missions trip we offer, regardless of the cost. And to the person, they almost always become more generous when it comes to reaching the lost locally.

It's that generous heart that resembles the heart of our Master, God, who loves every person on this planet so much that He... GAVE. Cultivate the giving heart of the Master, and you will find that you begin to see more opportunities to invite the lost around you to become the Son's Bride.

CHAPTER FIVE

STICK WITH GOD'S PLAN

*"T*hen Laban and Bethuel replied, 'The Lord has obviously brought you here, so there is nothing we can say. Here is Rebekah; take her and go. Yes, let her be the wife of your master's son, as the Lord has directed."* (Genesis 24:50-51)

A few years before I began one of my longest roles in ministry to date, the Lord spoke to me that He was going to bring me to serve in that capacity. It was a role that was elected by hundreds of my ministry peers at the time. And when the Lord spoke that to my heart and mind, I couldn't see how it could happen. I even told the Lord that there were at least eight to ten other ministry leaders who were better suited, more well-known, and more connected than me. So I just wrote it down, tucked it away in my prayer journal, and tried not to think about it. But God kept reassuring me that was the direction He was leading me. In fact, I was soon added to the leadership team.

Crazy as it seems, during the next few years, I watched almost every one of those other leaders (who I would have expected to be chosen before me) move far away or take on other ministry roles which would keep them from serving as the leader of that ministry. Sadly, some even lost their ministries due to moral failures in their lives that none of us saw coming. One by one, they were removed from consideration.

After a couple of years, I was elected to serve in an assisting capacity for that very role. But the day I was elected to serve as an assistant, I had more than one person come to me and ask if I was ready to be the next leader in that area of ministry. I fumbled around with my words because it was so awkward. I was simply happy to be on the team and serve our leader, and there were still others who seemed more gifted and qualified than me to serve in that role. So I just did what was asked of me, and I left the rest up to God.

A year passed, and just a few days before the annual meeting of my ministry peers, our leader contacted me to say that he was stepping away to follow the Lord's leading to another ministry. Then he suggested that I should pray about whether or not the Lord might want to use me to serve as the leader of that ministry if I happened to be nominated and elected. I took the weekend to fast and pray about what the Lord had spoken to me more than three years earlier and what now seemed to stand right in front of me. It looked like it could really happen.

The events over those next several days were complicated, and it appeared I might not even be able to attend the meetings as planned. Not being there could possibly have made it highly unlikely that I would be chosen. It looked as if the perfect storm was forming to prevent what it seemed like the Lord had spoken to my heart, even though it had looked like He was working everything together that way up to that point. Yet, in what felt like a moment, the situation rearranged, and worked out for me to be there. In the process of that meeting, I was nominated along with three of my friends. Unexpectedly, two of them told me privately that they knew the role was not for them, but they felt like they were supposed to be part of the process.

When the time came for the vote, it took several ballots. That year, the team facilitating the meeting was using a computer and video projection system for the first time to show the results of each ballot. At one point, there was a mistake between what the actual count was and what showed on the screen to everyone, and it looked like someone else was way ahead of me in votes. My heart sank until the mistake was immediately mentioned and the correction to the numbers was made. A couple votes later, our lives changed when we were elected to serve in that role the Lord had spoken to my heart about more than three years earlier.

But what if I had not stayed engaged in that ministry? You see, at the time, I was the lead pastor of a small, but growing church. I served on our local area ministers' leadership team. I was a representative for my alma mater in our state. And I served on the team for another department in our denomination. I was trying to do all I could to serve the Lord in whatever ways I saw. What if I had chosen to put more effort into those other areas and ignored God's plan?

At one point during those few years between God speaking and reality happening, the leader of the other denominational department I was serving with suggested that I was stretched too thin, and he felt that it would be wise for me to focus my attention in one area rather than serving in multiple areas. I thought he was about to ask me to give more focus to his area of ministry, but, instead, he encouraged me to move toward the other area; the one God had spoken about to my heart. He had no clue what the Lord had spoken me, but he thought he saw God doing something in my life, and he wanted to help me. So since he was a true friend, he nudged me to go in the direction it looked like God was leading; even if that meant taking me away from serving him. So I took his advice and decided to stick with God's plan.

I could have walked down many different avenues, but there is nothing like walking in the will of the One who created you. It certainly won't always be easy, but it will always be better than the alternative. And when you walk in the will of your Master— reaching those where He sends you and inviting them to be His Son's bride— there is no denying that you are on His mission. When God is at work in your mission, everyone can see it, and no one can deny it.

The servant could have gone other places to look for a bride for Isaac, but his master asked him to go to *that* place. The servant could have tried to find a bride from a different family than the one Abraham suggested, but that wouldn't have been his master's heart. Instead, he stuck with his master's plan. It was the right plan. It featured the right place, the right people, and the right timing. And he was the right guy to carry out the plan.

That became obvious to everyone involved. What his master knew and believed, others began to recognize: this mission was God's mission. This servant was more than Abraham's servant. He was God's servant. The plan was God's plan, and the bride God wanted for Isaac was clear.

Rebecca knew it. She probably knew it the moment the servant started showering her with gifts after she had worked so hard to water all his camels. She may have somehow known it before she offered, and that is what motivated her. Not that she thought she would become the bride of a wealthy man's son, but that somehow this day was different... this servant was different... this moment was different. Perhaps somehow she could sense the Divine plan for her life intersecting with this man's mission.

Laban and Bethuel knew it. They even said as much. They realized that they as mere men could no more stand in the way of what God wanted than to stop waves crashing on the shore or stop the sun from rising each day. All they could do was acknowledge God was up to something that involved their family. Somehow, they knew they needed to go along with what this servant was saying to Rebecca, even though it meant their daughter and sister would be moving hundreds of miles away in a time when there was no postal service and no quick, easy means of travel.

And the servant knew it. What Abraham had known in sending his servant, the servant was discovering for himself. God was truly in this, and it was a good thing he had stuck with his master's plan instead of going his own way. He had chosen rightly to go where his master sent him. He had chosen wisely to take those camels and that amount of gifts. He had chosen well by asking God to help him on his mission. Now he was seeing that others could see God's hand on him, on his mission, and on his master's family.

What I didn't know that morning when the Lord spoke to me those years before He brought about the fulfillment of that season in ministry for us is that He also spoke to Angela around the same time. She just had not told me. Oh, it wasn't in exactly the same way, but He showed her nonetheless. I'll never forget the day when I said something to her that hinted around at what the

Lord had put in my heart while we were driving down the road by ourselves, and we both revealed to the other what we thought the Lord might be up to with our life. Just knowing that someone else saw that God was in it also was reassuring. Yet, we didn't dare voice that, and couldn't do anything to make it happen. But along the way there were these confirmations that just kept coming that let us know we should stick with His plan.

The day came when we announced to the church we were serving that we had been elected to serve in this other ministry assignment. Interestingly, our leaders were not surprised. They said that though they were disappointed, they had seen it coming and saw God's hand on us for that work. More than once, we heard that same thing reiterated by other ministry friends. It was like no one could deny that God had set it up for us.

Those were amazing years of fruitful service in God's Kingdom for us, and we loved that season of ministry. But what made it great was that it was God's plan.

When you walk the path God lays out for you... in the way He lays it out for you... in the timing He lays out for you... and just stick with His plan, you will find that you are more successful at inviting the souls in front of you to become His Son's loving bride.

Know this: He has a plan for you. It's the right plan. You may wonder about His plan. It may seem like there is another way. You might even wish there was a different way. I would encourage you to stick with His plan. You may not see it at the moment, but since He hand-crafted that plan, it will be evident to others when you work that plan that He is with you. Make it your goal to stick with His plan, and you'll see that He sticks with you to make you successful at leading the people to Him who He sends you to reach.

Chapter Six

Stay On Task

"T hen they ate their meal, and the servant and the men with him stayed there overnight.

But early the next morning, Abraham's servant said, 'Send me back to my master.'

'But we want Rebekah to stay with us at least ten days,' her brother and mother said. 'Then she can go.'

But he said, 'Don't delay me. The Lord has made my mission successful; now send me back so I can return to my master.'" (Genesis 24:54-56)

I don't want to completely peg this on guys because that would be an overgeneralization... and personally embarrassing for our gender. Yet I know it has happened to me multiple times, and I have generally only heard of it happening with other guys. Particularly husbands. Wow, this hole I'm digging just gets deeper and deeper. So let me just say it about myself:

I have been known— possibly on more than one occasion— to forget the very thing I went to the store to get.

I am a go-er by nature. I like to go. If someone's going, I want it to be me. If others are going, I want to go with them. I like going. I've never met a shopping trip on which I didn't want to go. Don't tell anyone, but I can out-shop Angela on any given day. So I never mind when there is something that needs to be picked up at the grocery store or good ol' Wally World. Even if I've been out all day and just got home, I am just as happy to crawl right back in the pickup truck and roll down the road to get whatever ingredient is needed for whatever Angela is cooking up, or whatever item is needed for something the boys are working on at the time. It just doesn't bother me. Like Chick-Fil-A, it's my pleasure to go get them whatever they need.

Occasionally, another item or two will be added to the list, you know, since I'm going anyway. This would include a few other essential items that were kind of needed or would be needed, and this would save another trip just to go get those things. No problem, add them to the list. It's my pleasure. I love my family and want to bless them. That's what good husbands and dads do; we love and serve and bless.

When I get to the store, I start working the list. Now, I usually just make a list of the extra things that were added because I totally know in my brain what the main item was that I went on this excursion to get in the first place. And as I work the list, I might happen to see one or two— or seven— other items that I think we probably need. So I add them to the cart. I gladly wheel all around the store, smiling at folks and saying, "Howdy" (because we live in Texas), picking up items... some requested, some maybe not so much. Sometimes I will even call or text to see if there is anything else we need before I head to the checkout. Angela typically assumes that I am an adult who knows the primary purpose of his trip to the store. She is kind enough not to insult my intelligence and ask me if I remembered to get the only item I **_HAD_** to get on that little trip to the store. She might ask about the other items, but usually not that one because she trusts me to go get what I went to get.

So I be-bop through the checkout. I grab my little plastic sacks of all the stuff I picked up, and I head to the truck. Never once does it cross my mind to look in those little sacks to see what I got. I shove the receipt in my pocket or wallet or one of those plastic bags, load the stuff in the truck, get in, start it up, and drive home listening to some 80's Christian glam-rock or a suspenseful Christian fiction audiobook.

I walk in the door at home, so proud of myself for being such a doting husband and father, and I set the plastic bags on the counter in triumph. That's when Angela asks in which bag she can find **_THE_** item I went to get. And that's when it hits me: I forgot the main purpose of my trip. I didn't buy the very item I went for in the first place.

Sometimes, I don't even reply. I just hang my head, turn around, wave goodbye, take my walk of shame back out to the truck, and head back to the store.

Now you would think that after this had happened a couple of times in life, I'd learn my lesson. But it happened again just recently. Usually, after one of these mindless faux pas, I begin to make sure that any list for one of these trips *begins* with the very item needed. And when I call or text to see if anything else is needed, I specifically mention the item is in the cart. And when I checkout, I want to scan it first to make sure I got it.

That plan works well for awhile. Then I start to relax a little, and I don't think I need to put the main item on the list anymore. I mean, how could I forget the very thing I went to get?

Someone reading this right now, please say that I'm not the only one who has done this. Like raise your hand in the air and say out loud that I am not alone in this embarrassing act of forgetfulness. Thank you. Let's commiserate.

Let's be real... that's embarrassing enough. But if you think that's embarrassing, how about when we forget that the very reason the Lord leaves us on this earth after we become a part of His Son's bride is so that we can invite others to become the bride for His Son? It's the *one thing* He asked us to do.

God: "No matter where you go, no matter what you do, just remember to ask them to be My Son's bride."

Us: "Sure thing. Absolutely! Would never forget that is the prime objective."

We would never forget. Right? Of course not. Until we get distracted by a hobby. Or our work. Or a relationship. Or... or... or. Don't get me wrong. I'm not beating you over the head here. I'm saying that it is really easy for every last one of us to get caught up in this present phase of life and forget that we are on a mission with a sole purpose. People— some of whom mean well and have good intentions— can be like shiny objects distracting us from successfully going after what we came for and returning to our Master with said bride in hand.

The experience for Abraham's servant was no different. He knew he was on a mission, but others were not making it easy. Hospitality was the rule of the day in that culture at the time. The way you showed respect for people was to extend hospitality. So Laban and Bethuel were extending significant honor and hospitality to the servant.

On a couple of the trips I've been on to Israel, we have visited tourist experiences which have been designed to show what hospitality would have been like in Abraham's time. It begins with a warm greeting and welcome. You're invited as a guest to come into the tent to get out of the heat, to sit down, and to rest. While you talk with your host, you are served tea. If the host would like you to stay, more tea is served. In fact, they will just keep filling your cup every time you empty it. (They must be from the South.) If the host likes you well enough, or believes you deserve to be shown even more respect and honor, you are then offered a meal. Again, they will keep filling your plate as long as you keep emptying it. If night has fallen, you are invited to stay and get some rest before you head out again. And a gracious host might compel you to stay again the next day for more hospitality. Their goal is to make you glad you stopped there and sad to leave.

So what the servant experienced was completely normal. They were showing him respect. They were recognizing his master. They were expressing gratitude for the generosity the servant had shown toward them all. And they were not about to be out-done in the way of generosity.

But I don't think that is all there was to this. Mama probably hated to see her baby girl leave the nest. The whole family realized that once she left, they were not likely to see her again. Regardless of their motives, they tried to keep the servant from leaving and taking Rebekah back with him right then.

They're like, "Take a break. Cool your jets. It was a long trip here, and it will be a long trip back. There's no rush, no need for this urgency. Relax. You can leave next week."

But while others would have told him it's okay to take a break, Abraham's servant stayed dialed-in as to why he came. He remembered that his assignment was not just to find or identify a potential wife for his master's son. His assignment was to go, find the one, and bring her home to the son to actually *be* his bride. And since he stayed on task, he didn't let the objections or emotions get in the way of his mission. He had one assignment, and he wasn't about to forget it.

This is what we do when we stay at it with people till they accept Christ, and then we walk with them in discipleship so that they don't fall away. That takes a pretty big dose of staying on task. It's easy to identify lost people in this world. Everywhere we look, we see them. They exist on other continents across the world, and in other yards across the street. We can identify them at work, at school, and even at home. We might even see them while we are on one of those trips to the store to get one item that we must not forget.

Yet our mission is not just to identify the lost. It is to do all we can to show them the love and blessing of our Master, who desperately wants them to be His Son's Bride, and to stay focused on our task. Our mission is not just to tell them, and then walk away. Our mission is to do our part to try to bring them to Heaven with us. Sometimes that means a little extra effort. Sometimes that means not giving up on them when others say it would just be easier to leave them there if they don't want to go on the journey with us. But our mission isn't our own. It is the heart of our Master. It is His longing to see His home populated with as many as will become His Son's Bride. We simply have to stay on task.

Want to hear something ridiculous? Just now, while I am in the middle of writing this chapter about staying on task, I picked up my phone to look something up, and I almost got distracted with some article headlines that caught my attention. That's how easy it is. I'm writing a chapter about staying on task so that you can be encouraged to reach more people for Jesus, and I almost dropped the ball myself. Here's the thing: forgetting souls is far more important than forgetting the chocolate chips or parmesan cheese.

So make a list. Right now. Put those people on the list who you know you need to reach with the Good News of Jesus. Stay on task in prayer that they will turn toward Him. Stay on task looking for those opportunities to share Him with them. Stay on task when it's easy and when it's difficult. Stay on task. Remember, you just have one thing to pick up on your way to Heaven, and it's them.

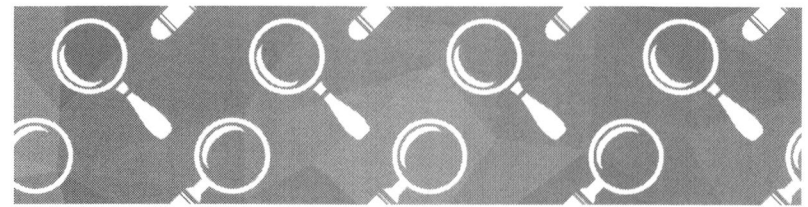

CHAPTER SEVEN

PRESENT WELL

"So they called Rebekah. 'Are you willing to go with this man?' they asked her.
And she replied, 'Yes, I will go.'" (Genesis 24:58)

Will Rogers is credited with this pearl of wisdom: "You never get a second chance to make a first impression."

He was right. I remember very clearly wanting to impress Angela. I realized she was one of those out-of-my-league kind of girls, but I was determined. I remember going home with her and a friend one week-end while we were attending college. Her dad invited me to pray over one of the delicious meals her mom cooked while we were there that weekend. He must have sensed that I would feel the need to impress, so he gently reminded me before I prayed that we didn't need to intercede for all the missionaries at the moment, just ask the Lord to bless the food. I took that hint, and kept it short, sweet, and easy to beat.

Then, as Angela and I began dating, there was another one of those moments. A guy who lived on our hall in the guys' dorm on campus was serving as a youth pas-tor at a local church about forty-five minutes from the university. He invited me and a couple of other guys to come preach a youth revival at their church. I was so excited. I told Angela and a few other friends about the opportunity, and they decided to go the night I preached to support me. In an effort to remain transparent, I went to serve the Lord and help my friend, but I also hoped that Angela liked my preaching. She didn't tell me till we were further on in to our relationship and more serious about spending our lives together, but she said she went that night to see what my preaching was like and if she could stand listening to it every week for the rest of her life. No pressure.

The truth is, we are all making impressions on the lives of those around us whether we know it or not, whether we want to acknowledge it or not. And those impressions can play a part as to how people respond to hearing about our Master's Son.

In 2003, Thom Rainer shared a statistic from his research which showed only 2% of Christians invite people to go to church with them. What is crazy is that Carey Nieuwhof shared in 2021 from his research that he had discovered 82% of people would come to church if a friend simply invited them. Most would move toward considering our Master's Son if we would just invite them to get to know Him a little, but most of us don't invite.

So a large part of the problem in getting people interested in knowing our Master's Son is that we just don't invite them to go with us. But there may be another challenge we need to overcome as well, and it is that sometimes we just don't present well. In other words, the way we approach life and sharing Jesus with others just isn't, well, inviting. The good news is that this is easily fixable. A slight change in our attitude can create a big change in our actions which translates into greater opportunities for people to say "yes" to Jesus.

I heard the story of one church who had a change of pastoral leadership. When the new pastor met with the church leaders, they talked about what had been effective at reaching the community for Christ and what the leadership might want to jettison because it just wasn't having the desired impact. One of the efforts was a giant Easter egg hunt held each year featuring thousands of eggs filled with candy. The community was invited, and a couple hundred kids would show up for the hunt. Thousands of dollars would be spent, along with plenty of volunteer time invested, but none of those kids or their parents ever gave their lives to Christ or even stepped through the doors of the church after being invited. Why?

I'm convinced the world looks at many of our efforts and events in the church and senses a "sucker-punch" coming. Too often, we bait them with free food (we were actually having dinner on the grounds anyway), games for the kids (which is just part of what our kids church does every week), and live music (which is, in reality, just our worship team playing), and they get to the church only to find out that we basically just invited them to a church service where they are going to be pressured to give their life to Jesus. I'd be skeptical of us, too, if I was them.

I had a conversation with a pastor just yesterday, and we were talking about what is effective and what is not effective as far as outreach. I told him that while we have big days with said free food, inflatables, and maybe even a door-prize drawing, we try to encourage our folks to be clear that we are inviting their family, friends, and neighbors to a church service where we believe they will experience God in a powerful way and then have fun afterward. As for outreach, though, what has been most effective at drawing people closer to Jesus are those out-reaches where we aren't even trying to get people to attend our church or sit in a service at all. What *has* been effective is our men coming together to serve widows and those with disabilities in our community by working on their houses, cleaning up their yards, and building wheelchair ramps. What *has* been effective has been the soup kitchen a retired couple in the church had the heart to start because they saw the needs of the undernourished in our community and wanted to bless them with at least one hot meal every week. That is what has gotten noticed in the community. Those are the kinds of efforts that have caused people to say they want to be connected with a church that loves and serves like that. *That* is what presenting our Master's Son well in our context and in our community looks like.

Abraham's servant had done his best from the first moment he arrived to present well. He had spoken graciously to Rebekah, and when she answered his prayer by offering to water his camels as well as give him a drink, he blessed her with tangible gifts of appreciation. He expressed interest in who she was and in her family. When he met the family, he blessed them with gifts.

The servant paid honor to God, to his master, to Rebekah, and to her family. He presented well those who had sent him. I don't know if they brushed their teeth back then, but if they did, I'm sure he did. I'm sure he did his best to make a good first impression because, as

Will Rogers would famously say four thousand years or so later, you don't get a second chance.

A number of years ago, I was helping a church who was currently without a lead pastor in their search for the person who would fill that role. We went through a handful of résumés, prayed over them, and discussed the potential of each applicant. As we came to one applicant, there was something that one of the board members brought up that really caught my attention. They said, "In the times that I have seen this person, it just bothers me that they always seem to look sloppy. It doesn't matter whether they are wearing jeans and a t-shirt, or a three-piece suit. They just don't look sharp. They don't present well. And I know that probably seems trivial, but when guests come to our church, I don't want them to think the whole place is sloppy based on our pastor's appearance. And it's not about the style of clothes. I have seen other ministers wear a track suit and look sharp."

Let me keep it real. I did think initially that it sounded a little trivial. Don't judge a book by its cover and all that. But as a guy who really tries to think through what his book covers will look like, I know it actually can matter. Someone may or may not decide to buy one of my books based on what the front cover looks like or what the blurb on the back cover says. We all make first impressions, and you can't get a do-over on those. So I sat up and took notes that day on what that board member said. I, too, stand in front of groups of people and declare who God is to them and tell them how much He loves them. But if I don't make sure my hair is fixed and my clothes look sharp... if I don't choose my words wisely and open with something that catches their attention... why would I think they would respond positively when the most important moment comes at the end of the message?

People have a choice. Once we have earned the opportunity to share Jesus with them, they will have to decide for themselves if they will go on the journey with us to be the bride for our Master's Son. And what's crazy is that it might hinge on whether or not we presented our Master and His Son— and even ourselves— in the best way possible.

How do we make Jesus sound to those around us? What do they think about Him based on the way we talk? What do our actions in life tell them about how real and special and wonderful He is to us?

If we say we are sold out to Him, but we don't make attending His house with others a priority, our neighbors will take note that our vehicle sits in the driveway on Sundays just like theirs. If we listen to and tell crude jokes around the water cooler or in the break room at work, why would they want to listen to us talk about living for Christ?

But if we give generously to real, felt needs in our community, they will take note of that. And if we give our time to serve at the local soup kitchen or pregnancy care center for single moms, that will register with them also. And if we go the extra mile to lovingly help them in their time of need, how much more likely is it that they will respond positively to the Gospel when a moment opens up for us to share Jesus with them?

This doesn't have to be big or difficult. Smile more often. Say "Hi" to people in the store. Yes, maybe even fix your hair, or at least put on a cool hat. Put on make-up if that's what helps you. Maybe stop to consider if your clothes match. I know it seems ridiculous, but we want to be the kind of servants the Master can trust to present well so that people will want to come with us to Heaven.

Then take it to the next level. Speak words of encouragement, hope, and life to everyone you meet. Pave the path with early words that will set the stage later when it is time for them to make a decision.

Want to crank it up a notch? Serve, volunteer, give. They'll see that you must have a good Master with a loving Son. Who knows? They might actually start to believe you mean what you say.

When we present our Master and His Son to people around us in the right way, they will be far more likely to respond, "Yes, I will go." They will want to be the Bride for the Son. And in the end, that's the goal.

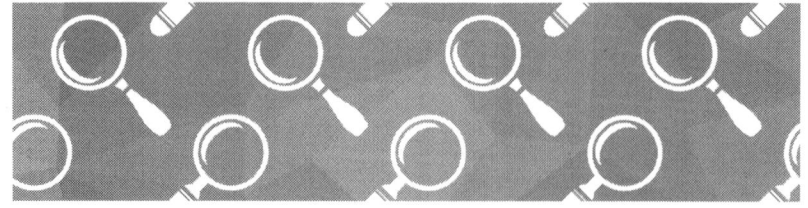

CHAPTER EIGHT

FINAL REPORT

"Then the servant told Isaac everything he had done." *(Genesis 24:66)*

In the fall of 2014, I embarked on a health journey along with five or six other guys under the guidance of a friend who was a health coach at the time. I was tired of coming home from my 9-to-5 desk job and being too tired to wrestle with our two young sons. I was also tired of standing on platforms in front of hundreds or thousands of people and feeling insecure about my physical appearance. You can call me lazy or vain, but those were my two main motivations for getting healthy. So when my health-coach friend invited me to gather some guys and let him take us on the journey, I agreed.

With my goal clearly in front of me, I truly applied myself. I haven't had a carbonated beverage since that time. We transformed the way our family eats, and during that season of training, I tracked everything that went in my mouth via an app. I exercised five or six days per week, and I even tried to make sure I got the right amount of sleep most nights in order to optimize my health. During that quest, I lost twenty-four pounds and got into the best physical condition of my adult life.

As part of our training, we not only watched videos and stayed in contact with our coach individually, but each week we gathered on a video conference call as a group. On that call, the coach would have each of us report how we were doing on the quest. Then he would randomly select one of us and show our app results— which featured everything we had eaten and how often we had exercised for the week— to the entire group. Talk about accountability.

At first, I was nervous that mine would be chosen because I wasn't sure I had done well. But as the journey continued, I became more and more confident because I was beginning to see the results of everything we were working to accomplish. I still remember the first time I went into a store the day before an out-of-state event where I was supposed to be speaking, and I was able to buy a smaller size shirt than I had been able to fit into in years. Soon, I began to look forward to the video conference calls, and I wasn't worried anymore because I knew I was doing what I was supposed to be doing, and I knew it was working.

So when it came to the end of our several-month health quest together, I was well-prepared to give my final results to our coach. I had met and exceeded my goal for weight loss. I was stronger than I had ever been. I had energy to out-play our sons. And I was able to stand confidently in front of crowds, knowing that I was living a disciplined life in as many areas as possible.

I didn't have as much weight to lose as some of the guys. In fact, a couple of times throughout the journey my weight increased as I built a little more muscle. Some of my friends were battling some real health challenges and just had more to lose than me. So I couldn't really compare myself to them, and our coach didn't want us to compare ourselves to each other. In fact, some of them had not done as well as they had hoped they would. Yet all of us had made progress. In the end, our coach just wanted us to let him know how we had done with what we needed to do. And when the day came to wrap up our intensive program, I was glad to be able to say that I had done my very best along the way.

That's the heart behind this book. When we one day stand and give our final report, our hearts should rejoice to give it because we know we have done the very best we could to complete our assignment.

It had probably been at least a month— probably more like six weeks— since Abraham had given his most trusted servant the assignment of securing a bride for Isaac and the servant had departed to accomplish it. That may not seem like a long time, but times were much different then than they are now. There were no texts or calls to let someone back home know he had arrived. There were no emails to tell them the good news that God had paved the path for him and led him to just the right young lady for Isaac. There weren't even carrier pigeons to take back news that Rebekah had said "yes" and that they were headed home.

As the servant covered each of the laborious hundreds of miles with his fellow servants and the new bride-to-be in tow, he knew that he would have to give account for his mission. Had he succeeded? Clearly, he had Rebekah with him, and so that answer would be obvious. He had to feel good about that in his heart. How had it all taken place? He knew the Lord had helped him. He knew that he had succeeded at something he wasn't even sure he would know how to begin to accomplish when the assignment was first handed to him.

But Scripture says that he told Isaac everything he had done. Why Isaac? Well, Rebekah would soon be his bride. And as he told her family, Abraham had given everything to his son. So it was Isaac to whom he brought Rebekah. And it was Isaac to whom he shared how he had used his time and the family's wealth in an effort to bring the bride home to him.

The servant stood before the son and gave a full account of his mission. He probably talked about how Abraham had asked him to take on this mission, and how he had wondered if he was even capable of accomplishing it successfully. He may have described the tedious miles traveled on the backs of the camels which were packed with all sorts of symbols of Abraham's wealth. Surely, he told how he arrived and asked the Lord to help him know who the right young lady for Isaac would be by having her offer to water his camels as well as give him a drink of water. No doubt, his eyes lit up— and maybe misted slightly, you know from all the dust on the road home— as he told how the beautiful young Rebekah became the answer to his prayer. He had to have shared about giving the lavish gifts to Rebekah and her family, and he probably told how impressed they were. And the story wouldn't be complete without telling how Rebekah's family wanted her to stay a little longer, but he pressed them to let him bring her on with him so that his mission would be complete.

And then he brought the bride to Isaac as assigned. Imagine the joy in Isaac's heart. Can't you just see the smile spread across his face as the servant stepped out of the way, bowed low, swept his arm to the young lady behind him, and said, "Here she is, sir, your bride." Mission accomplished.

Job well done. That's what Isaac and Abraham had to be thinking. The servant had done exactly what had been asked of him, and by the grace and power of God, he had succeeded in bringing home a bride for the son.

I never really liked final exams or the day that reports were due in school. I still didn't like it when after a major event or activity I was leading, my boss would ask me to give a report of how things had gone and what the end results were. However, if I had done all my homework and checked off all the things I was supposed to do along the way, it really wasn't that bad. The final exam would be much easier. The research paper would be well-written and properly presented. I would have a printed report with how I used my time, what results were achieved, and how I stayed within the budget. I was able to look at those report cards or go into those meetings with a lot more confidence. No fear, just peace. No worries, just a knowing that I had done my best.

One day, you and I will stand before Christ Jesus, our Savior, and on that day we too will give a full account for how we used both the time He gave us and the resources He entrusted to us while on our mission. Oh, we won't be standing there to see if we get into Heaven or not. For those of us who have surrendered our lives to belong to Christ, that part was settled at the Cross and the empty Tomb. In fact, we will actually already be in Heaven when we give this account to the Son. We won't fear that moment because His Word says in 1 John 4:18 that fear has to do with punishment, and perfect love gets rid of fear.

On that day, we will stand before Him as the servant stood before Isaac. He will know our name, even if no one else does. He will be well-aware of our mission. He will want to know how it went and who we brought with us, for He longs to reward us for our faithfulness. Keep that in mind. God is out to bless us as His children. He desires to be good to you. That's grace: giving us what we do not deserve. Yes, He may have given us the assignment to help populate His eternal family, but He did it with a side benefit of desiring to bless us for accomplishing that assignment.

I don't know about you, but I can probably only count on one hand the number of people I have directly led to the Lord outside of a church service or other ministry outreach setting. I hope that changes, though. I've had the privilege countless times of being the guy who gets to invite people to respond to a message and commit their lives to Christ. And I have also experienced the joy of raising up other leaders who have gone on to win people to the Lord. But I want to do more. That's what is in my heart. When I stand before Him on that day, I want to be able to report gladly to Him that I did all I could with His help, and I was able to bring numerous people into His family to be a part of His bride.

Between now and then, I want the journey home to Him to be full of confidence and joy that I have done the best I could with what He has entrusted to me to bring as many souls into His family as I possibly could with His help. I want to be able one day to tell Him how I gave so that churches and missionaries could reach more lost souls for Him. I want to be able to tell Him about the times I stepped through an open door to speak a word of hope or life that would draw someone closer to Him. I want to be able to tell Him about the times I was able to write a book or a social media post that caught someone's attention and drew them back toward Him. I want to be able to show all the times I made sure not to close out a service without giving someone one more opportunity to give their life to Him.

The truth is, I'm giving that report either way. So I want to make the most of it. I want to make sure it's my "mission accomplished" moment. I don't want to dread that moment. I want to look forward to it with great anticipation because I know I have given it my best effort. I want to be able to bow low before Him, turn, sweep my arm back, and with great pleasure announce the multitudes behind me are those whom I was able to bring to Him to be His Bride.

The rest of the story is that you will give that report as well if you are His child. And I want you to be able to give a great one also. I want you to stand before Him on that day with absolute confidence that you gave it your all. I hope your report is full of the stories of how you were able in many ways to offer eternal life to many people who took you up on that offer.

We're giving the report regardless. We might as well live and love in such a way that we make it a great one!

CONCLUSION

#relationshipgoals
  #squadgoals
  #parentgoals
  #gamergoals
  #moneygoals
  #influencergoals
  #vacaygoals
  #lifegoals

Everyone has goals. We all want to accomplish something. You might see someone with an incredible relationship and have a goal of having a great relationship like them. Or you might know someone who has an awesome side hustle that you wish you could replicate. I would surmise that, for most of us, our goals come from seeing something put out in front of us at which we want to aim. That's the goal of this book: to give us an example for which we can aim.

I subtitled this book "8 **GOALS** For Winning Souls" for several reasons:

- One, it rhymes and I love a good rhyme. (I grew up listening to DC Talk and ETW.)

- Two, it rolls off the tongue easily. (Preachers love that kind of stuff.)

- And three, it helps people immediately know what the focus of book is. (Unless you're my mom, that's why you bought this book, isn't it?)

But there is one other reason, and _that_ reason is that goals are something we aim to hit. I told you from the start that I didn't write this book because I'm an expert on soul-winning, but because it is in my heart to make sure others get married to Christ, and I'm trying to do my best with that. My best may not always match up to someone else's, but I'm doing my best anyway.

A goal is something you aim for in life. It helps you know whether you are winning or not, whether you are succeeding or even getting close to succeeding.

I could have subtitled this book, "8 *RULES* For Winning Souls," but rules by their nature are all or nothing. You either get it right or you don't. Yet the truths shared in *this* book from *THE* Book are goals we should aim for in life. If you try to share Jesus with someone— even if you don't get all the words right, even if you fumble around nervously— He is so proud of you. He smiles at your effort. Maybe you didn't swish the 3-point shot, but you hit the rim... or at least the backboard... and you can get the rebound and try again. Maybe you'll be able to make the lay-up. These are goals, not rules.

Or I could have called it "8 *KEYS* For Winning Souls," and a key seems like a magical device that only certain people have. Only my family has a key to my house or vehicle. Only a few people at the church have a key to my office. Keys imply someone important has the ability, but others do not. And keys can be lost. That's just not the case when it comes to inviting people to marry their lives with Jesus. Any of us can aim at the goal and try. And in the end, it's not completely up to us whether they accept our effort or not anyway. Our part is simply to carry the message from our Master to the potential bride, and invite people to come along with us on the journey back home to Him.

So you may not feel like you have the oratory skills of Billy Graham. Or the compassion of Mother Theresa. Or the social media following of a major Christian influencer. But that doesn't mean you can't see the goal and go for it.

The truth is, God (the Master) chose you (His servant) to go find people to be a part of His family (the Bride) through Christ (His Son). Think about that. He chose you. He believes in you. He knows you have the connections and relationships needed with those around you to make an invitation they will want to accept. You. He chose you. You're the servant He believes is best-suited to reach the people around you. No one else. You.

It's not about rules. So don't feel like you have to always be perfect and have the perfect words or perfect methods in order to invite someone to know Christ personally. Do the best you can, and ask the Lord to help you be successful. He will honor that. He will utilize that.

He will add His power to that. And one day, He will celebrate that.

And it's not about keys. This is something every child of God... every believer... everyone who calls themselves His servant can and should be busy doing. If you feel like you need keys, remember that Jesus said He gave the keys to the Kingdom of Heaven to His followers. So, you've got all the keys you need. God is the One who grants us access to those who He is inviting into His family. Maybe He's given you access to high school kids in a classroom at school or pre-schoolers in a Kids' Church setting. Maybe He's given you a ton of online connections. Maybe He's given you access to a number of people through your work. Maybe He's given you all the patients on your floor at the hospital. Maybe He has given you more cousins than one person should legitimately be able to have in a single lifetime. Whatever the case, you have all the keys you need. Walk through the doors He has opened for you, and aim for the goal.

It's not about rules or keys. It's about goals. It's about our hearts. Do we have it in our heart to do what our Master asks of us? Are we willing to set aside our own accolades or agendas? Are we willing to partner with

God to see the lost around us and around the world come to Him? Will we be generous toward others? When difficulties and distractions come our way, will we stay on mission? Will we do our best and leave the results to Him?

When we stand before Him one day and give a report of our time on this planet, the goal is to hear Him say, "Well done, My good and faithful servant." (Matthew 25:21) If we have done our best to be Bride finders for Him, He will be able to say those words freely and easily to us.

My prayer for you is that the time we have spent together through this book has inspired you to simply try. I pray the Lord will open doors of opportunity for you to invite people to spend their lives with Him. I pray you try every chance you get to find a Bride for our Master's Son. You may have a long list of goals in your life. Today, I'm simply hoping that you'll add one more hashtag to your goal list. Until He comes to take us all home to be with Him forever...

#BrideFinder

TELL ME ABOUT IT

If this book has inspired you in even the smallest way to have a heart that wants to see others come to know Christ personally, I would love to hear how it has impacted you. And if you have had the privilege of helping someone become a part of the Bride of Christ through salvation, then I definitely want to hear that story as well. Hearing your stories inspires me. So share your story of how *The Bride Finder: 8 Goals For Winning Souls* has touched your heart by emailing me at:

allen@allenchapin.com

ABOUT ALLEN

Allen Chapin has worn many titles. To his favorite people in the world, he is known as husband and dad. Others call him son, brother, uncle, or friend. He has served as a youth pastor, lead pastor, university staff member, denominational leader, and traveling speaker. Once upon a time, he also gathered carts at Walmart and ran a register at Academy Sports and Outdoors.

His life purpose is to help people find and follow God's path for their lives through love, encouragement, grace, and hope. One way he does that is by serving as the Director of the Called Initiative for the South Texas Assemblies of God Ministry Network. That initiative is designed to identify students called to ministry, then coach them and connect them for an effective lifetime of answering that call.

Allen loves hiking to quiet streams in the mountains, watching his favorite NFL teams play on Sunday after-noon— after church and a good nap— and "homemade pizza and a movie night" at home with his family. His favorite food is peanut butter, and his favorite color is blue. Although, if you look in his closet, you'll see a lot more black and gray clothes than blue.

Allen has authored three other titles— *I Got A "D" In Leadership: Anyone Can Lead, The Upside: 150 Daily Devotions*, and *Listen*— with more titles to be released soon.

OTHER TITLES BY ALLEN YOU MIGHT ALSO ENJOY

You can find these other life-impacting titles from Allen on Amazon: